D1415161

Open Hearts

FAMILY

Open Hearts
~ FAMILY ~

By JANE SEYMOUR

RUNNING PRESS
PHILADELPHIA · LONDON

Books published by Running Press are available at special discounts for bulk
purchases in the United States by corporations, institutions, and other organizations.
For more information, please contact the Special Markets Department at the Perseus
Books Group, 2300 Chestnut Street, Suite 200, Philadelphia, PA 19103, or call (800)
810-4145, ext. 5000, or e-mail special.markets@perseusbooks.com.

ISBN 978-0-7624-4910-1
Library of Congress Control Number: 2012943242

E-book ISBN 978-0-7624-4918-7

9   8   7   6   5   4   3   2
Digit on the right indicates the number of this printing

Designed by Susan Van Horn
Edited by Cindy De La Hoz
Typography: Alana Pro, Gotham, and Filosofia

Running Press Book Publishers
2300 Chestnut Street
Philadelphia, PA 19103-4371

Visit us on the web!
www.runningpress.com

Dedication

*To our ever-growing family of friends and the
inspirational stories that they have shared.*

♥

*To my husband, James, my sisters Annie and Sally,
and our children and grandchildren,
who inspire me every day to keep an open heart.*

♥

*To my mother, Mieke, without whom
this book would not exist.*

Contents

The Open Hearts Family

I WANTED TO WRITE THIS BOOK BECAUSE "FAMILY" TO ME IS more than genetic. Fortunately, my genetic family is extraordinary, and we are very close—probably because post-WWII our parents were so grateful to have us and to be safe and alive.

But "family" is more than genetics. It's about the moments we have in life when we touch or are touched by another in times of adversity or challenge—when we open our hearts and souls and trust one another with our deepest feelings. These people become our sisters, brothers, mothers, fathers. They are our *Open Hearts Family*, the ones who share a special bond with us. It can be anyone, even an animal that brings peace and love into our lives.

This book celebrates not only the traditional family unit that our birth provides, but also the unexpected families that we create from the people we open our hearts to as we journey through life. Within these pages you'll read stories by me, contributions from those touched by the message of Open Hearts, and words of wisdom from some of the great thinkers of history. When we open our hearts, our family grows; so do we . . . and so can the world.

—Jane Seymour

Your Family of Origin

∾ Born Into Love ∾

To be born into a loving family is the most wonderful gift that any of us could wish for. Within the safety of its shelter, we are able to experiment and discover our strengths and weaknesses and to develop our spiritual, intellectual, and artistic expressions of self in an atmosphere of love, belonging, and tolerance. Through the wisdom passed onto our parents by their parents and ancestors we learn the lessons we need to live our lives fully and positively, and to try to make ourselves—and the world—a better place.

—Jane Seymour

My mother, Mieke.
This drawing of her
was done in the
concentration camp.

～ A Mother's Moment ～

Before she ever had children of her own, my mother Mieke was inspired by the women she cared for in a concentration camp in Java during World War II. It was a terrible place where the sickest were sent to die. The water was unclean, dirty bandages were reduced to rags, and there was no medicine or antiseptic. Tirelessly, my mother went among her patients trying to make them comfortable; kind words and a listening ear her only resources.

She became very close to one woman in particular who had a terrible cancer in her lower back. Her suffering was immense, but she gained strength at the thought of being reunited with her children. One day the woman asked an inexperienced nurse for a mirror, quickly used it to look at her wound, lost all hope, and died.

Overwhelmed by helplessness and despair, starved and exhausted by her own struggle to stay alive, Mummy took to her bed. Heartbroken, she had lost all hope, her youthful optimism destroyed by the realities of war. The Matron came to see her and demanded she get up and carry on. It was a pivotal moment: Would she succumb to her feelings of grief and helplessness or stand up for love and be of service to others?

My mother chose the latter, and from that moment on she looked for the positive in life, and determined that should she survive, she would become a mother herself and teach her children how to love.

—Jane Seymour

~ Masterpiece ~

The family is one of nature's masterpieces.

—George Santayana

∽ Fill Your Heart with Love ∾

My mother taught me that acts of kindness, love, and goodwill toward others makes your heart grow. If you always keep your heart open and fill it with love, there won't be room left for anything bad.

—Anna

∾ Shining Light ∾

EVEN THOUGH THE FAMILY I WAS BORN INTO WAS WROUGHT with abuse, I did have one shining light: my great grandmother. She was full of love and all things proper, polite, lovely, and decent—and I remember that she always wore her beautiful silver bracelet. I am ever fortunate to have my own family now. This breathtaking painting is of my beautiful children, and my favorite part is my daughters' charm bracelets. An armful of silver bracelets has become my signature, and my most treasured is the one I inherited from my great grandmother—it is a constant reminder of her love.

—Laura Anne Harlan

∽ Light through Darkness ∽

My mother and I always had a challenging relationship; we never saw the world or my life the same way. Though she was an accomplished artist herself, she stood in the way of me following my own passion for a career in the arts.

However, my mother succumbed to Alzheimer's Disease and our roles reversed. I have become her caregiver and decision maker, which she has had to accept. But a miracle occurred, too. Every time I visit my mother I act, sing, and perform the very arts that I was once denied but now pursue with gusto. My fairly unresponsive mother smiles with a twinkle in her eye. We have found another way to open our hearts to each other before it's too late.

There was a light through the darkness of my mother's disease. By the very nature of Alzheimer's, the past is erased. There is only the present, a time to be even more loving and compassionate.

—Annette Fox

∼ Rejoice ∽

Rejoice with your family in the beautiful land of life!

—Albert Einstein

∾ The Greatest Gold ∾

*A family with an old person
has a living treasure of gold.*

—Chinese Proverb

∽ One Size Fits All ∽

AS EVERY MOTHER KNOWS, CARRYING A CHILD FOR NINE MONTHS gives you a special bond from the very beginning; then, after birth, caring for that infant enhances the relationship a hundredfold. I am the mother of two special-needs young men, and I believe the extra care they require only deepens our connection. I can feel their emotional pain; somehow, I know how their minds work.

One of the many definitions of family, to me, is having that extra-sensory knowledge of your child that defies comprehension. But the mother/special needs child relationship doesn't have a monopoly on it. Anyone in any relationship can have it. It's a one-size-fits-all characteristic of family.

—Deborah M. Piccurelli

Jane Seymour

❧ Love Heals the Hurt ❧

My family has faced many heartbreaks—illnesses and tragic deaths. At times I felt like giving up. Then I would look at my four daughters who loved me and depended on me to be strong. As children they learned from my examples. I did not want them to give up and close their hearts. So I taught them when you open your heart, love heals the hurt. My daughters are now young women, graduated from college and living on their own. I cannot shelter them from the worries of the world, yet I know that I have shown them by opening their hearts, love will find a way in.

—Debra

～ Servants to Each Other ～

To maintain a joyful family requires much from both the parents and the children. Each member of the family has to become, in a special way, the servant of the others.

—Pope John Paul II

∾ Unspoken, Unbroken Bonds ∾

I was only twenty years old when my husband told me he was leaving me for my best friend. I thought about killing myself, even attempted to do so. Then the most wonderful thing happened: I found out I was pregnant. I found my reason to live—my little girl Ashley!

I could have let the past make me bitter—but instead I let it make me better. Now, twenty-five years later, Ashley lives four doors down with her baby boy! She sings like a princess and always keeps music in the heart of my grandchild. She keeps saving me; she just doesn't know it.

My Open Heart ring reminds me that the bond between mother and child can never be broken.

—Elizabeth

∽ Always in My Heart ∾

JUST OVER ELEVEN YEARS AGO, WE WERE ANXIOUSLY AWAITING our first grandchild. She arrived early, and we watched helplessly but hopefully as she fought courageously for eight days. But God saw fit to take her back to heaven, where we know we'll see her again one day. Her short time with us opened our hearts to all children. Losing a child has a special way of making children even more priceless to a person.

Our seven other grandchildren mean so much to us, but I wear an Open Hearts Angel necklace for our lost Korryn Elizabeth. She may not be seated at our family dinner table, but she is right next to my heart!

—Elaine

∽ Hearts from Heaven ∽

I was devastated when my mom passed away while I was pregnant with my daughter. They would never know each other. As my daughter grew up, she would always mention seeing hearts everywhere: heart shapes in her bread, a heart-shaped rock, a heart-shaped shadow. I finally realized it was my mom's way of letting me know she did "know" my daughter, and was her guardian angel. Now, instead of being sad on the anniversary of my mom's passing, we have a Valentine's Day-like celebration with lots of hearts, and we reach out to others, including those in shelters and those without moms—to share our love!

—Tonya

Jane Seymour

Your Family
of Choice

❧ When Friends Become Family ❧

At the outbreak of World War II, my mother Mieke refused the opportunity to leave Java and escape almost certain imprisonment in a concentration camp. She stayed behind for the love of a friend. One of her girlfriends was pregnant, and she didn't want to abandon her.

Against the backdrop of the horrors of war, my mother and the women in the camp forged lifelong friendships that could never be broken. They all vowed that if they ever survived the war, they would open their homes to each other and their future children.

They all kept their promise. Growing up, our house was filled with my mother's best friends and their children, and we visited them in their homes. We really did all grow up together, and I learned from a very early age that friends and family really can be the same thing.

—Jane Seymour

This was my mother's friend, Marijke. The drawing was done by a fellow prisoner of war while she and my mother were in the concentration camp.

Jane Seymour

∾ Chosen For Us To Be Family ∾

IN 2010, ONE OF MY BEST FRIENDS SUFFERED A SUBARACHNOID hemorrhage several months after giving birth to her fourth child. I had been blessed to be in the delivery room when the baby was born and when I heard it "did not look good," my heart hit the floor. My parents both passed away years before this, so I was no stranger to loss, but this was one of my best friends. She and I had so many things in common that we considered ourselves sisters.

Previously, I had thought the birth of the child was the ultimate bonding. Not so! When I visited her in the hospital, we bonded in a way that I will never forget. It was a night that sealed our friendship in my heart and made us more than friends. We became family.

She recovered, which is a great blessing in itself, but she also changed my views on friendship and its importance. You don't get to choose your family but you can choose your friends. I believe that some friends are chosen for us by God because they are meant to be family.

—Sherri Wilson Johnson

A Friend, a Second Mom,
∽ an Angel ∽

Sometimes friends become your family. My mother's friend, Lynn Webber, became my second mom. When I was a teenager, my mother was diagnosed with breast cancer and had her hands full taking care of herself, me, and my special-needs brother—especially after my father left us, and we were homeless. Lynn took us in and we lived with her for three years. During that time, my mom's cancer went into remission and she found a good job. I graduated from high school with Lynn's help, and my brother was well taken care of.

I'm not sure where we would be today if it wasn't for her generosity and compassion. Lynn will forever be a part of our family. She is my mother's "sister." She is my second mom. She is our angel and we are forever grateful for her open heart.

—Stacy Wendel

∽ It's Like You ∾

Whenever I love anything, it is because it reminds me of yourself.

—Lord Byron

A Magnet in Your Heart

There is a magnet in your heart that will attract true friends. That magnet is unselfishness, thinking of others first. When you learn to live for others, they will live for you.

—Paramahansa Yogananda

∽ Unconditional Love ∾

WHEN MY OLDEST SON, NATHAN, PASSED AWAY SUDDENLY on April 10, 2010 at the age of twenty-five, my friend John was there for me. He made certain that I was not alone on Mother's Day, and he helped bring some joy to my heart. Even in the midst of the worst time in my life, his compassion and caring for me made me feel what unconditional love is. My heart was broken from losing my son, but still able to love! That is the greatest gift that anyone can have: the love of a good friend.

—lancy

∽ No Greater Love ∾

Greater love hath no man than this, that a man lay down his life for his friends.

—John 15:13

∽ Look to the Stars ∾

The night sky was bright with stars. We were twelve-year-old school children of missionary parents in China. I was from England and Winnie was from the U.S. During WWII we were interned in a concentration camp surrounded by walls, electrified barbed-wire fences, and trenches. Life was cramped and often unpleasant.

One evening Winnie and I looked up and observed the constellation Cassiopeia—a gigantic "W" of stars in the sky. (My surname was Welch.) We promised that every time we saw it we would remember and pray for God's blessing on each other. That's a promise which we have kept over the years. We have remained like sisters throughout our lives, sharing times of joy and sadness.

—Beryl Goodland

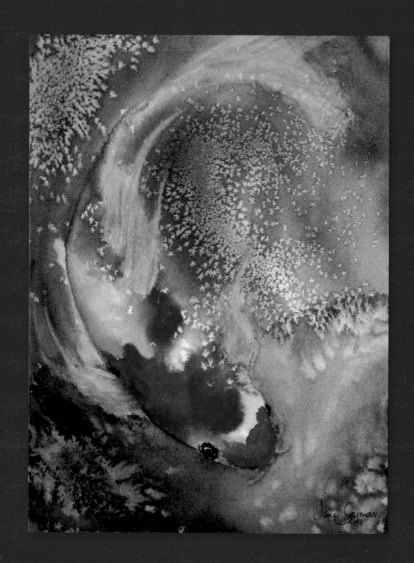

Jane Seymour

Finding Your Family

A photo of St. Catherine's Court, our home in England for twenty-three years, where all our friends and family gathered. This was taken by my son, Sean M. Flynn.

∽ The Family You Create ∾

Not everyone is lucky enough to have a great genetic family or instant circle of friends. But the beautiful thing is anyone can build their own family. There is an innate comfort in having a family that you have created. When you find someone to partner with, you also inherit their family and friends. Family continues to grow. It has no bounds. You can find it right next door or half a world away.

—Jane Seymour

∽ Extra Sisters ∾

When hard things happen to us in life we have two choices: bottle it up and live with the pain, or share these feelings with another, someone you trust, and find a way to process it and move forward.

One of our mother's greatest strengths was that she was able to open her heart to anyone. She could connect with others, listen to them, truly hear them, and become as close to another as it's possible to be. Because of this, our "family" was very extended.

So many young girls bonded with Mieke. They loved their own family, but chose our mother to be their closest confidant, and she in turn encouraged them to follow their hearts and passions. This resulted in us having a lot of "extra" sisters, and we love them all.

—Jane Seymour

∽ What Greater Thing ∽

WHAT GREATER THING IS THERE FOR TWO HUMAN SOULS than to feel that they are joined for life—to strengthen each other in all labor, to rest on each other in all sorrow, to minister to each other in all pain, to be one with each other in silent, unspeakable memories.

—George Eliot

∾ Every Heart Sings a Song ∾

Every heart sings a song, incomplete, until another heart whispers back. Those who wish to sing always find a song. At the touch of a lover, everyone becomes a poet.

—Plato

∽ My Husband's Gifts ∽

When I married James Keach I got the ultimate gift—not just his love, but also the way he immediately wanted to be a father to all of my kids. To this day he continues to be the one they come to for advice, even though in raising them he had the tough role of policeman and protector.

My mother Mieke and James' parents also bonded in a unique and wonderful way. My mother had been alone since my father's death many years before, but when Stacy and Mary Keach met her, they instantly included her in their world as family. They spoke almost daily on the phone from the U.S. to the U.K., and they even took cruises together. The three of them were a team. It was so beautiful to see: Mary and Mieke would howl with laughter like a couple of teenagers, and Stacy loved having two beautiful women on his arms!

—Jane Seymour

⁓ Grow Up in Greater Love ⁓

Smile at each other, smile at your wife, smile at your husband, smile at your children, smile at each other—it doesn't matter who it is—and that will help you to grow up in greater love for each other.

—Mother Teresa

∽ Love Letters ∽

ALONE AND IN A NEW CITY WITHOUT FAMILY OR FRIENDS, I prayed that I would meet someone nice. I knew that if I kept an open heart, "he" would find me.

Moving into my new apartment, I was given the wrong mailbox key. The mail inside was for someone named "Champion." The manager told me my new neighbor was a great guy, but out of town.

I was eventually introduced to Mr. Champion. We celebrated twenty-five years of marriage last April. When folks ask where I met such a great man and got such a cool name, I tell them I kept an open heart and just kept checking the mailbox.

—Kim Champion

∽ Love Will Find Its Way In ∽

Thirteen years ago, my sister Laura married a childhood friend. Scott was a lovely guy—fun loving, caring, and responsible. The first few years seemed like any other marriage; however, Scott had a troubled mind. While Laura was pregnant, Scott had a breakdown. He was on suicide watch at a mental hospital and diagnosed with bipolar disorder.

Their adorable baby Seth was born, and both Laura and Scott fell in love with him and tried to rebuild their lives together. Unfortunately, bipolar disorder is a cruel disease that cannot always be overcome. When Seth was seven years old, Scott tragically took his own life.

The devastation to my sister and her son did not stop with Scott's suicide. His mother openly blamed my sister and cut ties with her grandson. But Laura would not let anything destroy her spirit. She is raising her son to be kind and forgiving, and together they honor Scott's memory. Laura also became a resource in her community for others suffering with bipolar problems. She's dedicated to helping others navigate through their pain.

In the last year she has found an incredible man who adores not only her but her son too. She opened her heart when she thought she could never love again, and love truly did find its way back in.

—Cheri Ingle

∾ An Open Heart Overcomes ∾

I GREW UP AND LIVED WITH MY WONDERFUL GRANDPARENTS until their death. Then, when I was thirteen, I had to move in with my mother and stepfather. In their home I was so severely sexually abused that doctors said it would be impossible for me to have children.

It was hard to trust any man after that, but I could hear my grandmother encouraging me to not close myself off, to keep an open heart. After dating for eight years, my college sweetheart finally persuaded me to marry him—even though I might not be able to give him children.

I'm happy to say, we've been married for sixteen years now and have two beautiful girls. I lost three babies, so I often say I have two children here and three waiting for me in heaven, where I am sure my grandmother is watching over them. I am teaching my girls to have an open heart, just as my grandmother taught me.

—Genevieve

～ Home Is Where You Are ～

Steve asked me to marry him in 2009, during his second bout with cancer. I accepted, even though I knew that I would lose him, because I loved him no matter what. The first thing we lost though was our house—to a flood in 2010. I was fretting over it when he looked at me and said, "It doesn't matter. Where you are, home is."

Two weeks later he died. His last conscious words were, "Yes, I love you." An answer to an unspoken question.

Even though our time together was too short, he taught me to live and love, how to have joy instead of thinking "what if"—and how to live life without regrets.

—Hope

∽ Key to Prosperity ∾

A family in harmony will prosper in everything.

—Chinese Proverb

62

∾ I Love Her Till I Die ∽

There is a lady sweet and kind,
Was never face so pleas'd my mind;
I did but see her passing by,
And yet I love her till I die.

Her gesture, motion, and her smiles,
Her wit, her voice, my heart beguiles,
Beguiles my heart, I know not why,
And yet I love her till I die.

Cupid is winged and doth range,
Her country so my love doth change:
But change she earth, or change she sky,
Yet will I love her till I die.

—Anonymous

When Your Family Finds You

Women growing together

∽ The Flow of Love ∾

TO BE FAMILY IS TO OPEN OUR HEARTS—TO SHARE OUR experiences, feelings, and humor with one another. To unite and support one another no matter what. To be able to let go of issues, love one another, and forgive ourselves and them when times are tough.

As life goes on, we collect family by connecting ourselves to others in a united consciousness. We realize that nothing in life is more valuable than the flow of love between people. If you keep your heart open, your family will find you!

—Jane Seymour

∽ An Invisible Red Thread ∽

An invisible red thread connects those destined to meet, regardless of time, place, or circumstances. The thread may stretch or tangle, but never break.

—Ancient Chinese Proverb

∽ Room in Heaven ∽

Son, brother, father, lover, friend. There is room in the heart for all the affections, as there is room in heaven for all the stars.

—Victor Hugo

∽ Fostering Love ∾

Alice was my daughter Lucy's best friend at school. Alice's mother was very ill with cancer, so I would often pick her and Lucy up after school, and Alice would come home with us for supper and homework. Sadly, Alice's father abandoned the family, and after her mother died, things got worse. Her father met another woman, and when I asked him about Alice, he told me I was welcome to her.

That was it. I immediately set about formally adopting Alice. She became my daughter, Lucy's sister, and a much-loved member of our family. She worked very hard at school, put the setbacks in her childhood behind her, and is happily making a wonderful success of her life. We are so grateful that she came into our lives and that we have another daughter.

—E. M.

Jane Seymour

∽ Love is an Ever-Fixed Mark ∽

Let me not to the marriage of true minds
Admit impediments. Love is not love
Which alters when it alteration finds,
Or bends with the remover to remove:
O no! It is an ever-fixed mark
That looks on tempests and is never shaken;
It is the star to every wandering bark,
Whose worth's unknown, although his height be taken.
Love's not Time's fool, though rosy lips and cheeks
Within his bending sickle's compass come:
Love alters not with his brief hours and weeks,
But bears it out even to the edge of doom.
If this be error and upon me proved,
I never writ, nor no man ever loved.

—William Shakespeare, Sonnet 116

∽ Made-to-Order Family ∾

I was bitter that I had no children of my own, until I figured out that God was saving me for a special made-to-order family. A student at the high school where I taught needed a home, so I became a foster mother. My life seemed to fall into place with Deborah, who has been my daughter from age sixteen to forty-nine. We have a true mother-daughter relationship, and her son, Jacob (my grandson), is the joy of my life.

—Mary Ellen Snodgrass

∽ A Treasured Name ∽

Although I'd been his "daddy" since he was four years old, in the eyes of the law I was an interloper—just a step-dad. So when my son was twelve, and his biological father terminated his parental rights rather than pay child support, I welcomed the chance to formally adopt him. In my heart, he'd been mine for some time. I loved him and accepted his love without a legitimate stake in the family. But I wanted to be able to protect and provide for him legally as well.

He had to sign a statement that he agreed to the adoption and legally changing his last name. My wife and I were shocked when he asked if he could change his middle name too.

"What do you want it to be?" we asked. He looked directly into my eyes and simply said, "Michael." I felt the tears well up in my eyes as the statement hit me. "You want your middle name to be the same as my first name?" He nodded.

He is thirty-five years old now, and I still feel my heart flutter when I hear his full name called out. When he graduated high school, then college—it was a thrill for me knowing that he cared enough at the young age of twelve to take not only my last name but my first name as well. I will always treasure that.

—Michael Lee Joshua

Jane Seymour

The Working Family

Reaching New Heights
～ Together ～

We are not solitary creatures by nature. Humans have a need to build, to invent, and to reach for new heights by working together as a team. Those in the medical profession perform miracles for their fellow human beings every day. Teachers impact students' lives in immeasurable ways. People who serve in the Armed Forces create bonds that span a lifetime. Many times a family is forged at work.

—Jane Seymour

∽ War and Remembrance ∾

ONE OF THE FASCINATING PARTS OF BEING AN ACTRESS and finding yourself part of a group of people all working very intensely on an emotional project is that you become very close.

On the set of the television miniseries *War and Remembrance,* I recall meeting the German crew at a party to celebrate the beginning of our cinematic journey. I asked one of them how he would be able to handle working on this material. He laughed and said, "Oh it's just another film. No problem!"

It was especially hard for me as my mother had been a POW of the Japanese for three-and-a-half years, and my father, as a squadron leader in the RAF, had opened the gates of Belsen. Three of his close relatives died in concentration camps and he was always haunted by images of what he saw that day.

We worked on the series for nine months in five countries, depicting the horrors of Nazi-occupied Europe and the concentration camps. We were joined by survivors who had chosen to honor those they had lost by giving up their day jobs as lawyers, bankers, teachers, and rabbis to play background and relive those terrifying moments filming in the actual concentration camps they had survived.

At the end, we had all bonded through our mission to show the world accurately what had happened; and we had all changed. At the wrap party, the same German, a bear of a man, came to me completely broken and said, "You were so right. It's hard to see what our parents were involved with. We are a new generation, but we felt so horrified by what happened. It was too real."

I had to let go of my own feelings and open my heart to them. They had no choice; it was their parents' generation. I couldn't blame them. When you are touched deeply by shared events, and you communicate with open hearts and minds, you become family in this special bond. I'm sure he and I will never forget those nine months we spent together.

—Jane Seymour

∽ The Epitome of Love ∾

*L*ife has dealt me some pretty tough hands, but nothing compared to the end of my marriage. I thought I would never feel true love again until God placed a job in my lap: I became a Case Manager for adults with developmental disabilities. My clients are the epitome of love. The smallest of things brightens their day, and the love they radiate can be felt without saying a word. Seeing their happiness is a very humbling experience. They have turned my life around. Through them I learned that life and love live on, no matter what circumstances are thrown your way.

I'm still waiting on my "Prince Charming," but I've come to realize that love—true love—comes just when you need it most. I'm blessed to have sixty clients who remind me of this every day!

—Rebecca

∽ Go With Heart ∽

Wherever you go, go with all your heart.

—Confucius

∽ Rising Above ∾

WHEN THE OWNER OF THE SMALL COMPANY WHERE I WORK perished in a plane crash, everyone thought the business would go under. His wife assumed ownership, but she was badly injured in the crash, in the middle of adopting a baby from Vietnam, and had just lost her husband. We had eighteen employees, and we had a lot to learn really fast, but we wanted to make sure no one lost their job. It took sacrifice and a lot of teamwork, but we did it. In fact, the company is now growing and we just had to hire more people. Our secret? We all opened our hearts and became a family.

—Julia

～ Who Can Smile in Trouble ～

I love those who can smile in trouble, who can gather strength from distress, and grow brave by reflection. 'Tis the business of little minds to shrink, but they whose heart is firm, and whose conscience approves their conduct, will pursue their principles unto death.

—Thomas Paine

∽ Write It on Your Heart ∾

Write it on your heart that every day is the best day in the year.

—Ralph Waldo Emerson

∽ The Perfect Job ∾

When I was offered the job over a hundred other applicants, I felt like I won the lottery. It was a great place to work with great pay and lucrative benefits. I loved going to work, and I loved everyone there. However, I noticed that my special-needs son seemed depressed and not himself. My perfect job was taking a major toll on him. I knew what I had to do.

Tears streaming down my face, I gave my notice to quit. My supervisor understood. Family comes first.

I decided to surprise my son that day and pick him up from school. I told him that I was going to pick him up every day. His smile spread from ear to ear. That day, you'd think he won the lottery. I thought I had the winning ticket, but my son was the true prize.

—Mara Kim

The Family
Community

∾ An Online Community ∾

The family-oriented values espoused by the television series Dr. Quinn Medicine Woman *promoted much debate, bonding, and created lifelong friendships in the online community which are still active to this very day.*

Little did I expect that they would create a global online family, people who have become great friends and support each other in their daily lives. I'm always grateful to hear their Open Heart stories.

—Jane Seymour

∾ Family of the Heart ∾

FAMILIES COME IN ALL SHAPES AND SIZES. THERE IS THE birth family, there is the nuclear family, and there is the family of the heart.

For twenty-nine years, my husband and I have belonged to a dinner club. Those in the club have seen each other through the births of babies and the deaths of parents. We have weathered illnesses, celebrated each others' successes, and wept over the hurts that beset each of us. Our dinner club group is family in the best sense, bound by memories, by grief, and, most of all, by love.

—Jane Choate

~ Kisses for Kayla ~

When our daughter Kayla was diagnosed with a rare form of brain cancer at the age of seven, my wife Laurie and I were intensely private people who had no interest in sharing the details of our life with friends and family, much less complete strangers. We quickly found, though, that we needed to draw upon the reserves of friends, family, neighbors, co-workers, and many others to get through this challenge. We opened our hearts and developed a tightly knit yet widely expansive network of support.

When Kayla passed away in our loving arms, she left us in the arms of so many people who knew and loved her. We made the surprising discovery that in leaving us, Kayla somehow made our family larger, not smaller.

Living with (and eventually losing) Kayla taught us about the power of family—the family you are born with as well as the family you make by opening your heart to those around you.

—Eric A. Wenger

"Love"

∾ Generosity of Spirit ∾

Unhappy or tragic experiences in life can leave us feeling isolated, hurt, and unloved. It seems we have a reflex to close our hearts to prevent any more pain coming in, to put up barriers to protect ourselves from future hurt. The problem is that this "protection" also closes us off from what might heal us.

By opening our hearts we can escape from our self-imposed isolation and use our experiences to recognize others who may also be in pain. In reaching out to them, we rediscover the love and generosity of spirit in ourselves and in others.

—Jane Seymour

∽ Sisters of the Heart ∽

AT THE AGE OF THIRTY-TWO I HAD A MASSIVE HEART ATTACK and open-heart surgery. The doctors gave me one to two years to live, but I had not given up on my life and my family. I had young kids I wanted to see grow up and a loving man with whom I wanted to grow old.

I chose to live, and help others do the same. I started a support group for women with heart disease called Heart2HeartSisters. We started with five members and have grown to over a hundred! It's been thirteen years since my heart attack and I am blessed beyond words. I now have three grandchildren and another on the way. We need each other, and need to remind each other that there is always hope.

—Monica Whalen

∿ A Single Heart ∿

To give pleasure to a single
heart by a single act
is better than a thousand
heads bowing in prayer.

—Mahatma Gandhi

∽ It Makes the Heart Sing ∽

Rather than harbor resentment and dwell in self-pity,
I've put my time and talents into improving my city.
Through coaching and fundraising and donating my time
I've found that I can help others, out of the darkness climb.

Teaching kids new skills and rules, I've seen it change their lives.
All my time and effort is rewarded when a hug arrives.
We can all afford an Open Heart and the treasures it does bring—
Yes it takes some vulnerability, but oh how it makes hearts sing!

—James

J. Seymour

Furry Family Members

∽ All Creatures Great and Small ∽

Not all of our family members are human. Some have fur, feathers, whiskers, wings, tails, sometimes even beady eyes! We share our planet with peaceful creatures that will fill our lives with love . . . if we let them.

Animals can also help us connect with the human spirit. When animating the new series *This One 'N That One*, based on our children's books, James and I chose to represent our twin boys—the inspiration behind the idea—with twin cats. Cats come in all shapes and sizes, colors and temperaments, and we had twin cats of our own that we adored. My nephew, Charles Gould, recently wrote a book called *The Splendid Pig* that teaches children about living with an open heart through the adventures of a well-dressed pig. Life lessons are sometimes more gently learned when taught by an innocent creature.

—Jane Seymour

∽ Leading Me to Love ∾

I was pretty walled in. At age forty-two, I had never had a serious relationship and never thought I would. Seriously depressed, I adopted a poodle puppy. He changed my life by making me laugh at least once every day! While on our now habitual walk, I met a neighbor. We became friends, and then when I was fifty we fell in love and got married. Our Poo-boy is now fourteen and spoiled rotten. But he deserves it, don't you think?

—Marsha

～ Stashy ～

Our family cat, Stashy, is a rescued feral cat. As a wild cat we never expected him to be so open and loving with humans, as well as other animals. Recently he's opened his heart to a field mouse—his new best friend! He is one of the most loving animals we've ever known.

—Jane Seymour

J Seymour

∽ What We All Share ∽

ONE MORNING WHILE SITTING OUTSIDE WITH MY THIRTEEN-year-old dog, Cody, I noticed all the different types of trees. Some were dark and had heavy leaves; some were light with leaves you could see right through. I realized it was a lot like people: We are all different in color and size, but we all breathe the same air and look at the same sky, and we share a wonderful God who made us all.

Several days later we had to say goodbye to our little Cody. I knew that God would send us another little buddy to take care of. We found him online—a Cocker Spaniel that needed rescuing. Keeping your heart open even when it hurts can change anything.

—Donna Cullen

∽ Rescued by Love ∾

I lost my two best friends in 2007, within three days of each other—my mother and dog. I was devastated and didn't want to go on until I found Teddy Bear, a rescue dog. I knew it was meant to be because he needed me, or maybe I needed him more. We've been together ever since and I cannot imagine my life without him.

—Dawn

∾ Such Agreeable Friends ∾

Animals are such agreeable friends—they ask no questions, they pass no criticisms.

—George Eliot

∽ Captured My Heart ∽

Murphy, a little dwarf pet bunny, captured my heart from the first moment I saw him. He was like a baby to me, and comforted me through a difficult time in my life. He gave me back the love that I needed to be happy. Murphy brought me six years of joy and love. He will always be something special for me.

—Nadine

~ It Sings ~

A bird does not sing because it has an answer.

It sings because it has a song.

—Chinese Proverb

Our Human Family

∽ Connected by a Common Cause ∽

As members of the human family, we are all connected in some way. We see it in the unwritten laws of the universe that bring us together when we are meant to cross paths. We see it in our connection to the spiritual world and to each other.

Our world is expanding every day with new ways to reach out to our neighbors. We've opened our borders. Let's open our hearts and make sure to stay connected to one another.

—Jane Seymour

∽ Of One Family ∽

All men are children, and of one family. The same tale sends them all to bed, and wakes them in the morning.

—Henry David Thoreau

∽ The World Itself ∽

That one is mine and the other a stranger is the concept of little minds. But to the large-hearted the world itself is their family.

—Sanskrit Proverb

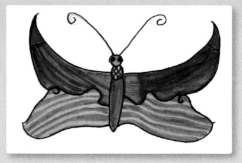

Drawing by Christina-Taylor Green

For the Love of
⌒ Christina-Taylor Green ⌒

ON SEPTEMBER 11, 2001, IN THE MIDST OF A GRIEVING NATION, a face of hope and joy was born into this world. Nine years later, on another day of inexplicable violence, that same little girl went to heaven.

Christina-Taylor Green was a remarkable nine-year-old. As a newly elected student council member, she was a natural leader, thrived on politics and public service, and wanted to help others less fortunate than herself. On January 8, 2011, Christina went to meet her local congressional representative, Gabby Giffords, who was speaking at a nearby Tucson supermarket. There, the unimaginable happened—a shooting rampage. Thirteen people were wounded and six were killed, including the youngest victim, Christina. Four days later, President Obama honored Christina's unfulfilled dreams saying, "I want to live up to her expectations." In the face of unimaginable sorrow, John and Roxanna Green opened their hearts. They directed their fury and passion into something positive: The Christina-Taylor Green Memorial Foundation. They've organized and supported numerous charitable and educational projects that reflect and embody Christina's interests, values, and dreams.

～ Child of War: Sarah's Story ～

How does a child of war come to America with nothing and end up becoming a nurse? With the help of new friends that become family. Teacher Kathy Paysen wrote this in honor of her one-time student and lifelong friend Sarah Boaz.

A child of war, Cambodia's own
Upon her heart she wore a crown
God, the witness to such pain
A motherless child in the rain

American shores opened wide
Loving thoughts in a world's tide
Feet pressed in freedom's run
Prayers like flowers of the sun

Healing hands from war's tether
Hate has burrs, love finds pleasure
A woman chiseled from war crimes
Sarah is now a nurse, love divine

Such is peace, American grace
Sarah's story, our human race

—Kathy Paysen

∽ Bound Each to Each ∾

My heart leaps up when I behold
A rainbow in the sky.
So was it when my life began;
So is it now I am a man;
So be it when I grow old,
Or let me die!
The Child is father of the Man;
And I could wish my days to be
Bound each to each by natural piety.

—William Wordsworth

∽ With Our Thoughts ∽

We are what we think.
All that we are arises
with our thoughts.
With our thoughts, we
make the world.

—Buddha

Art Titles and Descriptions

Page 2: Seymour, Jane. *Open Heart Family*. Mixed-media on paper, 10 ½ x 8 ³/₈"

Page 6: Seymour, Jane. *Country Sunflowers I*. Watercolor with pen and ink on paper, 7 x 4 ½"

Page 8: Seymour, Jane. *Anemones in Tall Vase #2*. Watercolor with pen and ink on paper, 9 x 6"

Page 10: Seymour, Jane. *Solitude*. Oil on panel, 12 x 9"

Page 13: Seymour, Jane. *Into the Woods (Sisters in the Meadow)*. Watercolor on paper, 20 x 14 ⅛"

Page 14: A Prisoner of War. *Portrait of Mieke*. Drawing on paper, 10 ¼ x 8"

Page 19: Seymour, Jane. *Shining Light (The Harlan Children with Bunny)*. Oil on canvas, 20 x 24"

Page 20: Seymour, Jane. *By the Bay*. Watercolor with pen and ink on paper, 9 ⅛ x 12 ¼"

Page 25: Seymour, Jane. *Romantic Red Roses*. Oil on canvas, 12 x 12"

Page 29: Seymour, Jane. *Red Ribbons* (detail). Watercolor on paper, 12 ½ x 16 ½"

Page 32: Seymour, Jane. *California Poppies*. Oil on panel, 10 x 8"

Page 35: A Prisoner of War. *Portrait of Marijke*. Drawing on paper, 8 x 8"

Page 36: Seymour, Jane. *Portrait of a Gardenia*. Watercolor on paper, 8 x 8 ¼"

Page 44: Seymour, Jane. *Sparkling Koi I*. Watercolor on paper, 12 x 9"

Page 46: Flynn, Sean M. *The Red Tree* (detail). Limited-edition Lambda C-print, 30 x 40"

Page 49: Ingle, Cheri. *Gabriella and Ruby*. Pastel on paper, 25 x 19"

Page 53: Seymour, Jane. *James*. Pencil drawing on paper, 9 x 9"

Page 55: Gould, Charles. *Balloon Love*. Color drawing on paper, 4 x 4"

Page 57: Seymour, Jane. *Summer Petals Bouquet*. Watercolor with pen and ink on paper, 6 ½ x 5"

Page 58: Seymour, Jane. *Magnolia at the Huntington Gardens* (detail). Watercolor on paper, 10 x 8"

Page 61: Seymour, Jane. *Mosaics from the South of France II* (Home). Watercolor with pen and ink on paper, 5 ½ x 3 ⅝"

Acknowledgments

Annie Gould, Sally Frankenberg, James Keach, Heather Maclean, Susan Nagy Luks, Cheri Ingle, Debra Pearl, Susan Ginsburg, Dick Guttman, Susan Madore, Jim Palmer, Ron Fujikawa

Our Family: Kalen, Danya, Sierra and Dylan, Jenni, Chris and Rowan, Katie and Brett, Sean, Johnny and Kris

Mary Ann Marino and Tiffany Stockton

All of my passionate art collectors, whom I have met in the galleries

Our Corporate Families: Kay Jewelers, Amini Innovation, Winward International, Wentworth Galleries, Guthy-Renker, StyleCraft, Innovative Artists

Running Press: Cindy De La Hoz, Susan Van Horn, Christopher Navratil, Craig Herman, Stacy Schuck

All my dedicated and supportive fans worldwide, who continue to inspire me by sharing their inspirational open heart stories